Cover design by Stephen Bailey
Cover layout and formatting by Marvin Rhodes, Jr.
Edits by Ellen Nicole Usher
Book editing by Tina Anderson
Published by Andre Renee
– Andree Renee Writes Publishing Co, LLC

Andre Renee Writes


Connect with the authors:
Facebook: @conflictcircumvention
Twitter: @RonChinaJax
Email: conflictworkshoppro@gmail.com

Later Lessons (Discoveries of Life and Love)
By: Ron (China) Jackson & Char Jackson

# Content

### *Prologue*

It is our sincere hope that this text proves to be of benefit to any and every one regardless of age or station in life. The majority of these writings could be categorized as advice concerning life and love that we would give our younger selves and/or counsel we would give to our own adult children.

As co-authors of this book and in our mid-forties, we've discovered love later in life after experiencing our own failed relationships and marriages. There's been plenty to reflect on. Combined there's a total of over 30 years of marriage and another 14 years of live-in relationships. We in no way consider ourselves as experts; however, given the magnitude of experiences, both good and bad, as well as mishaps, we've gathered our so-called PhDs in what not to do.

There were many life lessons we were given fair warning about from our own elders. However, much of this advice was given without meaningful context. This allowed for many of these cautionary tales to go over our heads until it was too late. It is our hope that this writing will find those in need of said advice and allow them to have a layman's understanding of many of our life's discoveries. While this information may not be new ideas or concepts for all, our ultimate goal is for whoever opens these pages to grasp and apply the necessary gems to fit their situation as this writing may give a different perspective.

## Lesson 1:
### *Understanding of Being "Evenly Yoked"*


It is taught that when two people are from the same religious background they have a better chance for a successful marriage. That would be true if we excluded the difference in environments in which the two individuals were raised. In our experience, two can be of the same religion yet have been raised in different environments/cultures within the home. It is due to this scenario that we look at being evenly yoked from a cultural perspective opposed to a religious one.

Ron: Being evenly yoked from a cultural perspective makes all the difference in my experience. It is often believed that individuals from the same religious or even ethnic background have a lot in common. While there may be some shared general commonalities, the cultural experiences of each, in the community and home, may be vastly different. While an individual from Antigua and an African American from the South are both considered "Black," their cultural experiences are not the same. While one may not be able to truly feel the vibe of a Luther Vandross groove, the other may not truly understand the spirit of Carnival. On another end of the spectrum, a "White" American raised in the South will have a completely different American experience than a Caucasian raised in California. The same can be said of two individuals raised in the same city and of the same race but with different economic status. In comparison, due to a shared culture within our homes as children, my current relationship has been able to thrive.

Although our families have different religious backgrounds, the cultural experiences and values taught in our homes were on the same accord. This commonality of culture and shared values has brought me a sense of peace I did not know in my past relationships. Many times being evenly yoked has nothing to do with religion; how one values money is an example. Have both parties grown up in a culture of saving and investing or was one brought up having a distrust of banks or only knowing of check-cashing services and payday loans? Has one party grown up in a home where friends were allowed to sleep over on the regular while the other was not allowed to have or attend sleepovers? How will these differences impact how you raise your own children? What conflicts may arise? Again, this is more of a cultural dynamic, as even individuals of the same religion can have different cultures within the home.

Let's take three families of the same race from the same neighborhood. One home is headed by a child's grandparents. Another is headed by a young married couple in their late 30s or early 40s, while the third is headed by a single parent. Needless to say, even if all homes follow the same religious beliefs, the overall culture in the homes will differ.

In an effort to pass this knowledge on to my younger self, my children, or anyone else, I would explain that although opposites may attract, as you get older and look for stability, it's all about commonality and being "evenly yoked," stressing that being evenly yoked has far more to do with common culture than religion.

Growing up I had a friend we'll call Grady. Grady is a Black male who went on to marry a Caucasian female. Grady was raised in a middle-class home by two hardworking, African American parents. During Grady's engagement and even after he and his wife took their vows, many questioned how and why this union was formed due to the Black and White differences. In a candid conversation, Grady told me that the way his bride was raised was far more in line with how he was raised in comparison to the Black girls he had dated. The cultural similarities in the homes in which they grew up in outweighed the cultural differences bestowed on them by society. Both grew up in two parent homes where they saw each parent go to work every day in their chosen profession and work together to establish a certain quality of life that included home ownership, financial responsibility, etc. While both witnessed this balance of teamwork, they also experienced the traditional playing of gender roles by their parents. These types of similarities drew the two together.

**Char:** I on the other hand was raised in a very strict religious household where I dare not date at all, period. Balance was not exercised in our home when it came to the outside (non- religious) world. Evenly yoked meant being of the same religion. It didn't matter how one was raised when they came into the religion. As long as both parties accepted the faith and its traditions, their union would be in perfect harmony as they were believed to be evenly yoked.

I was raised in a two-parent home with three other siblings. My parents were not of the same religion when they met, but my father brought my mother into his religious circle. While they were not initially evenly yoked religiously, they shared a common thread of growing up poor and fatherless with a communal understanding of what they wanted and did not want for their own family. They have been together/married for over 50 years.

My father was the breadwinner and my mother stayed at home to take care of four children. Everyone and everything had a place in our home. My mother prepared meals, did housework, and laundry while my father brought home the money and made sure we always had a dependable car and adequate housing. My mother trained us girls to be homemakers. This included sewing and ironing. My father taught my brother the "man's role," which consisted of working on the family car, lawn mowers, and painting the house. Inside the home, my brother only took out the trash. I left home going out into the world as an adult with a preconceived notion that I would meet and marry my own perfectly imperfect mate. To my dismay, life lessons and culture shock began. My first marriage was for children; my children's father would later pass away. My second marriage was due to loneliness. Both times I married men who were raised culturally different than I was. Both had come from fatherless homes with working mothers. They both felt that women were on an even playing field as men. I was raised to think that even if both adults worked outside the home, they still managed their respective roles within the home with the husband being head of the household and making the important decisions. I went into these marriages finding no "role" for me to play, hence being out of my element and consequently leading to disastrous marriages. Looking back, neither marriage had a chance as neither husband had experience as to what a two-parent home looked like or functioned as in my opinion. Not saying my thinking was right or wrong, but our ideas of what culturally our marriage and home should look like were not comparable.

# Lesson 2
## *Every Pot Has a Top*

### *(Different People Bring Different Qualities to and out of You)*

When I was a child, my beautiful and witty mother would notice different couples while we were out and about town. When, appearance wise, there seemed to be no rhyme or reason as to why these two people were together, my mother would shrug her shoulders and conclude, under her breath of course, that "every pot has a top." This was simply her sarcastic way of stating there is someone for everyone. We would laugh and move on with our current activity.

This has rung extremely true throughout my relationship journey. There were a lot of tops out there but none fit my pot. I think at times I would try to make men fit my pot by searching for common interests and trying to see things from their perspective even if it went against my own logic. I remember once I met a man who told me he was going to be a millionaire. I was intrigued until he reveled that he knew how to draw very well and was going to buy a million sheets of college-ruled notebook paper and charge a dollar per sheet featuring one of his original illustrations. After that and a few more unshakeable offenses, I ran.

I ran a lot and often from relationship to relationship finding that in each one I could not find my role to play. They would be financially stable yet insecure and possessive, or we would share the same understanding of family structure yet they would not know how to give and receive love.

This idea of every pot having a top is a simple one. In sort there's someone for everyone. However, for me, this goes a little deeper as I realized that different people bring different things to and out of you. We tend to think that people don't change. We live in a society that speaks of second chances but often moves differently. Do we really give rehabilitated criminals a second chance? When it comes to matters of the heart, we often move with this same notion. Sayings such as "once a cheater always a cheater" and "you can't teach an old dog new tricks" speak to this mindset. While there may be some truth to these dictums, I will combat this notion by saying *there's a top for every pot.* To expound, different people bring different qualities to and out of you. Just because someone moves and acts a particular way in one relationship doesn't necessarily mean they will behave the same in the next.

It isn't etched in stone that someone's interaction will be completely the same from relationship to relationship. Sometimes it's possible that a different person may bring a different energy to you and pull something different out of you. I've often heard and seen people speak of someone and admit they've never experienced, or even seen, what others may have encountered with the same person. Now these differences in experiences may be both positive and negative. Speaking from my own experiences, I've been on both the receiving and giving end of this modification. Without thought, I've moved totally differently in one relationship in comparison to another. While I may have consciously made an effort not to repeat some of the same mistakes from my past relationships, this difference in thought and communication was more a natural occurrence than a concentrated effort. The "every pot has a top" notion believes that some tops may not be as good of a fit for certain pots as others. The energy you bring to or receive from someone makes all the difference. Sometimes we may be forcing the top to fit for whatever reason. While no one wants to be seen

as a failure, or their relationship to be viewed as a negative

statistic, sometimes removing the top that doesn't truly fit

their pot makes room for the top that does fit to find them.

# Lesson 3
## *Age Really Is Nothing but a Number (When It Comes to Your Dreams)*

This lesson was inspired by a celebrity I reluctantly went to hear give a public lecture. While I have nothing against the gentleman, I just didn't see the benefit of taking time out of my day to hear him speak. This gives way to another lesson; you never know from where inspiration may come.

The name of the celebrity is not important, but his message and the inspiration of his message are. To paraphrase his monologue, age really is nothing but a number when it comes to your dreams. My understanding of this is based on my own experience. At the time I was 43 and in the beginning stages of what I now recognized as a mid-life crisis. Professionally and personally I was doing just "OK" and was in a rut. I was over 40 and not living the life I had always envisioned for myself. The fact that I was a lot closer to 45 than not, I had just about given up on my dreams and the life I wanted. I was in the beginning stages of *settling*. I'd always anticipated that by the time I was in my mid-40s, I would be where I wanted to be both financially and in my personal relationships. It was this luminary's talk of vision boards and affirmations as well as his own story that made me realize that I didn't have to *pack it in*. Even if it takes me another 10 years to achieve the quality of life I desire, to be able to spend the last years of my life, however much time I may have left, is well worth it. Not only is it worth it, as I apply the knowledge I've accumulated up to this stage of my life, but also the journey is so much more fulfilling as I'm able to appreciate and enjoy the small successes in a manner I wouldn't have been able to in my younger years. Again, age really is nothing but a number (when it comes to your dreams).

## Lesson 3.5
### *Age Can Be More than a Number (in a Relationship)*

Age may be nothing but a number when it comes to your dreams; however, when it comes to a relationship, age can be of optimal importance. Get too far ahead of yourself and you may find yourself taking care of your significant other and burying them before you guys even begin to really live, build, and totally learn each other. Date too young and you may find yourself raising your mate right along with your own children; amazing sexual gratification can only go so far. As with anything you have to find a balance.

Imagine sitting and talking about historic events and just reminiscing while your partner is looking at you with a blank stare or having to Google the topic. At times we get so caught up in the fantasy of love and happiness that we forget about common interests, goals, and communication. These are the golden nuggets that will allow a relationship to endure throughout sickness, health, and far into our rocking chair years. No one wants to grow to be old and alone. What better way to grow old than with a partner to whom you can truly relate.

# Lesson 4
## *What Women Want*

The answer to this question should garner me millions as this is an age old question that many have pondered for centuries. The reality is, the answer to this question is such a simple one that it amazes me that the answer isn't common knowledge.

In years of conversations and in my own relationships, I've come to realize that while it may be different from woman to woman, there is a common thread in the answer to this perplexing question. Being that each person has their own portrayal of what this answer looks like for them is the reason for all the mass confusion and uproar in the area of love and relationships. Now I could go on and on for the next 45 minutes talking about and rehashing the issue like one of those video links you click on in some social media platform, all in an effort to convince you why you need to buy something. If you're reading this, you've already bought the book. So what's the purpose? The answer to one of the oldest questions to ever plague man is simply *security*.

The issue is that many people don't know or have different definitions as to what security means to them. Yes, there may be some commonalities but the depths of what security is for one woman may be totally different from another woman's definition. One woman's classification of security may be shiny cars, fast money, shopping sprees with plenty of designer clothes, and handbags. Another woman may view a blue-collar worker with a "good job" and being *present* as a loving father as security. While yet someone else may deem a college educated, white-collar worker with a stable career, and varied financial investments as the only measurement of true refuge. Yet still another woman may view the independence of not having to depend on a man at all as the ultimate center of security… So the lifelong question, *what do women want*, may not be the question at all. The question men should be asking women and women should be asking themselves is, what is security to you/me.

# Lesson 5
## *Decoding the "Happy Wife Happy Life" Notion*

I recently saw a meme on social media that said, "Happy Spouse Happy House; Men Deserve to Be Happy Too." I chuckled as for years I felt the exact same way, but as I've gotten older, I very much agree with and understand the whole *happy wife happy life* concept. The problem with this saying, as with many things in today's society, is that there is no frame of reference surrounding it. The expression is just thrown out in the wind as some blanket Confucius wisdom. The foreground of this saying is just as much for women as it is for men.

The meme is correct; we as men also do deserve to be happy. However, what the saying *happy wife happy life* doesn't elucidate is how a woman's happiness should automatically translate into happiness for the man. Today's usage of the adage loosely translates to the notion that the man will have peace, i.e., no nagging or issues, as long as his wife is happy. On the surface that may be the layman's understanding, but from a more cognitive frame of thought, there's more to it.

Let's be honest. As men, we're not overly complicated. Our road to contentment is vastly less congested than after work traffic; however, there are particular attributes a man may want and need out of a relationship as no two men are exactly alike. Experience has shown that in a serious, loving, committed relationship, a woman learns her man on many levels and is more than capable of holistically nourishing him. Simply put, to make your woman happy is to ultimately please yourself. It's not about the avoidance of being nagged; it has more to do with your wife's happiness being the inspiration for her to naturally do things that make you, as her man, feel happy, wanted, and loved.

However, as mentioned in lesson 4, just as many people don't know or have different definitions as to what security means to them personally, the same holds true in terms of happiness. One can only define happiness for themselves.

Love a woman the way she should be loved and your house will be your castle, and you shall be King. Study her and give her all that you possibly can of yourself as a man, and she will glow and give you a lifetime of happiness. Not a guarantee, once again, no one is perfect. So always communicate and believe what you hear when communicating. Do not try to change anyone as people being themselves/comfortable in a relationship is of the utmost importance. You will know if she is your Queen.

# Lesson 6
### *Dealing with Loss/Emotions*

In a face to face lecture Dr. Denial Newman defined emotions as "Stirred up feelings caused by what you think." It's this thought on emotions that leads to my understanding of dealing with loss. Being that this writing is not focused solely on romantic aspects of relationships, the considerations in this lesson may be applied across the board when coping with loss.

As suggested by Dr. Newman, managing emotions is a cognitive process. While there is no sure-fire way to alleviate all grief associated with any form of loss, addressing it from a cognitive perspective is a skill set I would have definitely benefited from in my younger years. Moving with an understanding that everything has a *beginning, middle, and an end* has allowed for acceptance during times of loss.

This concept may seem a bit cold and harsh but the reality is there are many situations in which we are allowed to dictate the middle and ending. For instance, one may be in an argument and engage in behavior that may forever alter the direction of a relationship. It is this action, which is guided by "stirred up feelings caused by what you think," that may usher in an ultimate ending of said relationship. The term *ultimately* is used as said behavior may define the *middle* of the relationship, as there is often a buildup prior to its ending… Applying this concept of everything having a *beginning, middle, and an end* cognitively eases the process of coping with loss in general. As we may miss those who are no longer with us, this understanding aids in ultimately accepting said loss. While use of this concept may not erase any of the stages of grief, it does aid one getting through each stage and ultimately reaching the stage of acceptance.

I have lost so much in my lifetime: a child and a husband. What I've learned and will share with others is that you do heal and the sun does shine again. Also, do not let anyone tell you to *get over it*. Take as much time as you need.

# Lesson 7
## *Things Are Not as They Seem*

There have been certain ideas, experiences, and memories that I've held on to since my youth. I would have laid down my life with the belief that my understandings were in fact accurate. Imagine my astonishment to realize that at the age of 40 +, what I always thought I knew and understood wasn't so.

When I was in the 7th grade, my grandmother left our home and moved over 500 miles away. Over the years I have struggled with this to the point that I'd have dreams for months that she had died. Due to this sudden and tragic experience, I spent many years of my early adult life dealing with issues of abandonment. Later in my adulthood, I realized that my grandmother hadn't abandoned me. She'd actually moved to take care of my aunt, her youngest child, who was struggling with drug addiction. Now being an adult and a parent myself, I can only imagine the pain my grandmother endured during that time.

Now that I am a middle-aged adult, I've become privy to conversation and information from my mother and uncles that I previously had no access to. Be it my lack of life experience not allowing me to comprehend, or the adults in my life wanting to keep my mind free of adult issues, I now realize that many of the ideas and conclusions I have clenched to for years simply were not so.

Keeping with the theme of *advice I would give my younger self and/or counsel I would give to my own adult children*, things are not always what they seem. Life has a way of presenting you with truths that can change your entire perspective… The young man I was at 23 is not the person I was at 28 or even 30. Just as the father I was at 33 is not the same father I was at 42. The commonality of these different ages is experience and perspective. For those who may not understand, as my elders used to tell me, "just keep living" as things are not always as they seem.

This is a very true statement. There are so many songs I sang as a child that once I became an adult and realized what I was singing, I was appalled. LOL. When you become of age 40ish, you will go through a period of reflection about your childhood. There will also come a time when you will reflect on parenting experiences/skills. I encourage everyone, at some point in their life, to have a conversation with their children, parents, and close family members and reminisce. It is good for the soul and you will hear stories you have forgotten. Listening to your children, you will hear stories you have never heard before and learn things about them and yourself you never knew; it's therapy. It's a time for families to rehash the past, laugh, and get clarification on misunderstandings you never knew existed. It's all love in the end.

# Lesson 8
## *It's Not Necessarily All Good*

The idea of staying together for the sake of the children has been touted in movies, TV shows, and society in general since forever. This idea often comes across as a big fairytale but isn't always as nice and neatly wrapped as it may seem. Coming from a two-parent home where I was raised with three other siblings, I saw our parents love each other dearly. Their love for each other was almost to a fault, as they were often so immersed in their own issues it seemed that they forgot to show us love. It often felt as though they were the only ones in a relationship and the kids just came as part of the package.

Even though I know my parents truly loved one another, there were things that happened behind closed doors that led me to believe my parents should have gotten a divorce. This leads me to wonder how and why couples stay together for the children. Looking back on my experience growing up with two parents who loved each other yet having to endure all I encountered as a child, I can only imagine someone growing up with parents who do not share a true love for one another.

Having encountered people who have stayed in marriages and relationships for the sake of the kids, I've heard tales of parents pitting children against the opposing parent. I've also witnessed children learn firsthand how to be deceitful, manipulative and disloyal. Having children grow up resenting the fact that they were put in the middle and forced to endure years of unhappiness is not an ideal scenario. Contrary to popular belief, there are certainly cases when divorcing or separating is in the best interest of the child's well-being.

Separating may make way for the child to fully experience each parent and develop their own relationship with each parent, as opposed to constantly having to *put on a face* and disguise their misery. Ultimately children see the misery regardless. In many ways, this forces them to pick sides, as they are often left to sort out their immature feelings of like and dislike on their own. Separating and becoming agreeable co-parents allows the child to develop a healthy understanding of regrouping and how to communicate in spite of differences. It also helps in a child's understanding of how to maneuver in different environments, i.e., mom's house versus dad's house. Now if the two parents are able to co-parent as true friends, that's even better for the child because they get to witness a great, mature relationship between two people with a common love, their child.

# Lesson 9
### *Food for Thought*

I often read yet seldom comment on the many different posts and conversations I see on social media. The surprising thing about many of these posts is that they seem to all share a commonality. I'll take this opportunity to address what I see as the overall theme of many of the posts.

One may not be living up to their full *relationship potential* based on their mate and not even recognize it. If your mate only requires you to perform at a mediocre level, you may perform and become comfortable living and performing at that level and never realize your true potential. However, if your mate requires a higher standard of performance, you will either rise to the occasion or step away completely.

The fear of being alone (basic need of belonging) often times is the reason one may be leery of putting too much pressure on their mate to live up to a desired *relationship potential*. This may ultimately lead to a lifetime of unfulfillment for one or both parties, thus introducing issues of self-esteem and resentment that may linger long after said relationship has expired.

This train of thought goes back to our idea of "different people bringing different things to and from you, and every pot having a top" from lesson 2.

As far as observing posts and conversations on social media, I've noticed a common theme in terms of both men and women not being able to find what they desire in one person… I recall taking my children to Build-A-Bear when they were younger. For those unfamiliar, Build-A-Bear is a store that allows you to build/create your own stuffed animal. You're able to customize each toy with its own scents, sounds, and other amenities. This is what appears to be taking place in a lot of relationships today, the *Build-A-Bear mentality*.

Both parties, male and female, seem to be guilty of this as different individuals seem to serve a different, yet particular purpose in their lives. One person may make them laugh uncontrollably but unfortunately a good time is all they have to offer. Another person may stimulate them mentally but has no sense of humor. Yet, a third or fourth person may stimulate them sexually or bring about financial security but is unable to arouse any of the other senses or yearning. Many people are simply taking their favorite attributes from each person to create their own idea partner. Not only is this unfair to all parties that are unwillingly involved, but also it can be taxing to the person conducting the orchestra as they often have to stay "on" in an effort to delicately manage this balancing act. With this being said, I also believe the act of finding someone that checks all, or at least most of your boxes, goes back to the idea of "different people bringing different things to and from you, and every pot having a top" from lesson 2.

# Lesson 10
## *Trying to Understand It All (in Layman's Terms)*

The "Branches of Love" sounds like a love song by Barry White or Luther Vandross. In reality, very few people find this tree, let alone are able to climb it. The base or the trunk of the tree is wide and solid; it symbolizes the love everyone wishes for, the love that we experience and hope to hold on to in any relationship. Underneath the soil are our roots, which encompass things that have shaped us, i.e., ancestors, family legacy, values, favorite foods, movies, teachers, friends, and all the fond memories that serve as our foundation. These roots also hold our religious views, as well as pains and disappointments. The branches of this tree represent other relationships we have. Some branches are weak with no leaves and are ready to break with any small gust of wind, while other branches are strong and full of life. The leaves represent attributes such as love, caring, empathy, etc. Some branches may even become overwhelmed with so many leaves (attributes or emotions) that you can barely see

the branches.

While it's been noted that love is like a tree with many branches that encompass many things, for the sake of simplicity I've come to view relationships as an LLC. Not to say that I view them as a business where I personally can't be held accountable for my wrong doings… Experience has shown me that romantic relationships must be comprised of three main ingredients in order to be successful; this being said, LLC stands for Like, Love, and Communication.

We often view the word like as a simple one but its impact is enormous. Just as you may like a certain food or type of car, there are certain people you like. And just because you genuinely like being around and interacting with someone doesn't mean that you love them. The same holds true on the opposing end; just because you love someone doesn't mean you like them. For an example, let's all take a look at our own families.

We all have a family member or members we deem as not good people for whatever reason. Often times these are family members we do not "like" yet being that we share a common history, memories, etc., we love them as family nonetheless. The same is possible in a romantic relationship on the opposite spectrum. It is possible to love someone and later come to realize that you no longer like them, yet there's a sense of love that remains. Just as in a family, this may be due to past experiences you've encountered with said individual. As previously stated, the act of like or liking someone is needed to secure success in any romantic relationship.

For the sake of not being redundant, I won't overly address the definition or value of love in the LLC. However, I will remind you of the importance of many of the branches that comprise love, i.e., trust, respect, etc., while taking a closer look at caring.

In all actuality, to care/caring for someone should be able to stand on its own. If someone cares simply due to love, caring becomes conditional. Dare I say there is a deeper level of caring that is not tied to love? A caring act done simply out of love, specifically in a romantic relationship, may possibly serve as a selfish deed, as performing such an act aids in fulfilling one's sense of belonging within said relationship. Just as one can perform an act of caring for someone simply out of concern in absence of a loving relationship, an act performed simply out of caring has more to do with the person being cared for than the one doing the caring. With that being said, let's focus on the C of the LLC: communication.

Hearing that you must have good communication in order to secure a successful relationship may seem cliché. Also advice on how to communicate may seem even more hackneyed. The reason for this travesty is simply that we are not taught how to effectively communicate. In an effort to correct this issue, we must begin with the purpose of communication... The purpose of communication is to exchange information. Herein lies the problem as there is often a groundswell of personal information, be it emotional or cultural, that we do not privy others to. Being intentional or not, this in turn causes us to become insignificant communicators. Not to mention we lack openness in accepting perspectives different than our own. Lack of effective communication brings about resentment, as it allows one to wallow in their own feelings, thoughts, and perceptions – all of which may be falsehoods in comparison to their mate's interpretation. For more information on effective communication, diversity, and conflict resolution please visit

As stated previously, this information may not be new ideas or concepts for all. Our ultimate goal is for whoever opens these pages to be able to grasp and apply the necessary lessons to fit their situation as this writing should be categorized as advice we would give our younger selves and/or counsel we would give to our own adult children concerning life and love. With that being said, a lesson we've come to realize toward completion of this book deals with the connectivity of relations. In a perfect world, all parties with whom you share connectivity will relate and connect with one another. The reality is all parties may not connect nor is it necessary for them to do so…

The relationship you have with others is just that, *your relationship*. Everyone you have ties with does not have to have ties to one another. While it may be tempting to try to unite everyone, it isn't realistic that everyone will hitch. While you may be the common thread between all, you must remember that fruitful, long-lasting relationships are often built over time and arrive from various experiences and commonalities. Simply put, it is hard enough to shape your own relationships, let alone define the relationships of others given differences of culture and thought process. Many times the best that can be expected is cordiality and mutual respect. If it is indeed meant to be, time will foster a sense of community between all, thus allowing everyone to forge their own bond.